ALARA Inc. Monograph Series

No. 5

Action Research Engagement: Creating the Foundation for Organizational Change

Wendy E. Rowe, Marie Graf, Niels Agger-Gupta,

Eileen Piggot-Irvine and Brigitte Harris

School of Leadership Studies, Royal Roads University

Monograph Series edited by Eileen Piggot-Irvine
Royal Roads University, Victoria BC, Canada

Published by

Action Learning, Action Research Association

2013

2nd Reprint 2020

Biographical Statement:

Wendy E. Rowe

Wendy E. Rowe, Ph.D is an Associate Professor in the School of Leadership at Royal Roads University (Victoria, Canada). Her academic work focuses on management behaviour, teamwork, change management, organizational behaviour and development, program evaluation and research methods. Her research areas include health system change, action research design, resiliency and leadership. She is a credentialed evaluator with the Canadian Evaluation Society and has completed more than 200 evaluation and action research studies across domains of education, juvenile justice, corrections, substance abuse and other addictions, and mental health. She has published several articles on organizational evaluation and has produced more than 100 study reports. Her latest publication is *Transforming Stress in Complex Work Environments: Exploring the Capabilities of Middle Managers in the Public Sector*, published in the *International Journal of Workplace Health Management, March 2013*.
Wendy.Rowe@royalroads.ca

Eileen Piggot-Irvine

Eileen Piggot-Irvine, Ph.D is a Professor of Leadership at Royal Roads University (Victoria, Canada) and an Adjunct Professor at both Griffith University (Brisbane) and Unitec (Auckland). She was formerly Director of the New Zealand Action Research and Review Centre (NZARRC), Director of the New Zealand Principal and Leadership Centre (NZPLC) and senior lecturer at Massey University, and Head of the Education Management Centre, at Unitec. She has published four books, multiple book chapters, approximately 50 journal articles and presented too many keynotes etc to count. In the last six years she has directed 11 evaluation contracts (several at a national level) and recently won a national Canadian grant to lead a team of researchers investigating the impact of action research.
Eileen.piggotirvine@royalroads.ca.

Marie Graf

Marie E. Graf, MA is an experienced executive leadership facilitator and coach. Her 35+ years of experience focuses on transition in the workplace, executive development coaching, and the evolution of change (personally, professionally, and within/throughout organizations). She has held leadership roles with the Province of BC, Crown corporations, and in the private sector. She is an associate faculty member in the School of Leadership Studies, Royal Roads University (Victoria, Canada) and was awarded the Kelly Outstanding Teacher Award in 2012. She is a founding member of the High Technology Crime Investigation Association B.C. Chapter and of the Project Management Institute Victoria, B.C. Chapter. She received an Excellence in Project Management award from the B.C. government in 2003. Marie.Graf@royalroads.ca .

Niels Agger-Gupta

Dr. Niels Agger-Gupta, Ph.D. is an Associate Professor in the School of Leadership Studies at Royal Roads University (Victoria, Canada) and a consultant and researcher in organizational change, cultural & linguistic competency in health care, Appreciative Inquiry, and program evaluation. He has been affiliated with Fielding Graduate University's Institute on Social Innovation (2003-07), California Healthcare Interpreters Association (2000-02), Calgary

Regional Health Authority (1992-2000), and Alberta Multiculturalism Commission (1987-1998). Niels.Aggergupta@royalroads.ca

Brigitte Harris
Dr. Brigitte Harris, Ph.D is the Director of the School of Leadership Studies at Royal Roads University (Victoria, Canada). She has used evaluation, and engagement strategies to lead positive change and organizational transformation in post-secondary, private sector, and government organizations. Her research interests are in ethical development of leaders, organizational change through stakeholder engagement and action research, and leadership education. Brigitte.3harris@royalroads.ca.

Acknowledgement

The authors wish to acknowledge the contributions of, Niels Agger-Gupta, Brigitte Harris, Marie Graf and Marilyn Taylor in the formulation of key concepts underlying the current paper, some of which were articulated in the Organizational Action Research Model developed for students in the Master of Arts in Leadership Program at Royal Roads University (Rowe, Agger-Gupta, Harris, & Graf, 2011).

Table of Content

Tables

Figures

Abstract

The Action Research Engagement model (ARE) describes principles and implementation steps of an initiative that helps organizational stakeholders increase their engagement and 'readiness' for the change phase of action research. ARE is a cyclical process of inquiry, dialogue and deliberation that aims to lead organizational members to: shift in attitudes toward change; open understanding of different points of view on issues and opportunities for change; identify potential approaches to challenges and barriers; generate vision/goals, strategies and actions; and lead to viable action plans for sustainable change. This preparatory ARE model is based on theoretical premises about the role of dialogue and participation in inquiry processes in generating engagement, commitment and 'readiness' for change—all of which are necessary and foundational to a successful change intervention. Two case studies illustrate the ARE model and processes.

Keywords: Organizational change, readiness for change, action research, engagement, dialogic methods.

Action Research Engagement:
Creating the Foundation for Organizational Change

Introduction

Success in organizational change efforts is frequently poor (Beer & Nohria, 2000). In a recent McKinsey global survey of organizational leaders, only a third reported successful outcomes (Meaney & Pung, 2008). Armenakis and Harris (2009) concluded in their review of 30 years of research on change initiatives that failure to achieve success with change goals is often linked to employee motivation to embrace the change. Among many factors related to employee motivation is lack of readiness associated with beliefs, attitudes and intentions among organizational members (Armenakis, Harris, & Mossholder, 1993).

Along with Armenakis and Harris (2009), and Kotter (2007), this article argues that lack of employee motivation for change can be directly or indirectly related to a failure to personally engage the organizational members early on in the change process in a way that builds their belief in, and contribution to, the change goals. Following on from this proposition, the early engagement of stakeholders in the planning of change is accomplished by involving them in an inquiry activity that: leads to shifts in beliefs about the change initiative; opens them to different points of view; increases their understanding of issues; and identifies challenges, barriers and opportunities (Akgün, Byrne, Lynn, & Keskin, 2007). Additionally, through early engagement stakeholders begin to deal with what change means for the organization in terms of new or revised vision/goals, strategies and actions, and leads to actions plans for sustainable change intervention.

In the authors' experience, the grounding of a change initiative in early stage elements of thoughtful inquiry, collaboration, dialogue and reflection often mitigates resistance and enhances progress on implementing a change agenda. Such elements are strongly associated with action research principles, which the authors have articulated in the Action Research Engagement (ARE) model: a preparatory model designed to enhance organizational stakeholder acceptance or readiness for the change phase in action research. In particular, this model aims to clarify how organizational members view and analyse the issues associated with change, and how they entertain and support the implementation of solutions or strategies for improvement.

In this paper, gaps and shifts in thinking about change, the readiness factors that support successful organizational change, and the significance of creating organizational stakeholder engagement in the change process, are described. The principles of action research, including how an action research process can be deployed within an organization to engage stakeholders to catapult change, are then introduced. Finally, the specific processes of the ARE model are described, followed by two cases to illustrate the model.

Organizational Change Thinking: Gaps and Shifts

Much has been written about change. Anderson and Ackerman Anderson (2001), for example, describe three types of change. *Developmental* change involves incremental improvements to the existing structures. *Transitional* change—also called transactional change (Burke & Litwin, 2009; Gardiner, 2006)—requires replacing the existing structures and processes with something new to the organization but not fundamentally changing the character or purpose of the organization. *Transformational* change refers to changes in the identity, cultural norms and 'purposing' of the organization. Of the three types of change, transformational change is most interesting to us because it involves a radical shift of 'culture, behavior or mindset . . . a shift in human awareness that completely alters the way the organization and its people view the world, their customers, their work and themselves' (Anderson & Ackerman Anderson, 2001, p. 39). However, such a radical shift often creates ambivalence (Piderit, 2009) and the greatest need for early engagement by those impacted, in order to avoid escalation into resistance (Lines, 2004; Szabla, 2007).

What actually changes in an organizational change process might be defined differently at many levels (London & Sessa, 2006; Torbert, 2004); for individuals (the personal level), within a group of people (group or team level), or across the whole community or organization (the system level). Table 1 illustrates the complexity of what might change at each level in a transformational context versus a transactional context. The transformational changes at the personal and team levels need to occur before outcomes at the system level can be manifested.

Table 1. *Levels of Change for Transactional versus Transformational Change*

Type of Change	Personal Level	Team Level	System Level
Transactional Change	Job behaviours; how tasks are performed on the job	Team behaviours; how teams do tasks	System reporting structures and procedural processes
Transformational Change	Values about how to do work; paradigms about goals/purpose for individual	Team values about work, roles, relationships with others	System dynamics and purpose/values relative to learning, people relationships and sustainability

Further to this point, Torbert (2004) articulates levels of learning linked to change when it occurs through active inquiry for the individual inquirer (1st level change), for the participants in an interactive group (2nd level change), and across the whole community or organization (3rd level change). Torbert (n.d.) asserts:

> We have shown statistically that leaders who voluntarily engage in intense action inquiry activities during their workdays and special retreat workshops transform to later action-logic . . . [i.e., double and triple loop learning]. We have also shown statistically that CEOs engaging in at the Strategic-Systems Oriented action-logic and later are the only ones who are reliably successful in promoting organizational transformation. (para. 5)

In the following sections of this paper, the complexity of the relationship between inquiry and transformational organizational change is unravelled and the need for leader as well as key stakeholder early engagement is illuminated.

Huy and Mintzberg (2003) offer insight into the change process by urging that a focus on dramatic change (imposed and driven from the top) should be tempered by the realization that effective change often emerges inadvertently (organically or through evolutionary processes) or develops in a more orderly fashion (systematic change). By implication, change can also be seen as unplanned or planned (goal focussed). In terms of planned change, Van de Ven and Poole (2009) provide a summary of theories of change processes utilizing teleological theory as the underlying premise behind change that proceeds towards a goal or end state. In their terms, 'Development [is] a repetitive sequence of goal formulation, implementation, evaluation and modification of goals based on what was learnt or intended by the entity' (p. 865). According to Van de Ven and Poole (2009) teleology stresses the purposiveness of the entity but that the goal is not a fixed end state, rather it continually evolves and is socially constructed.

Having a goal orientation in change is relevant to the ARE model and is, therefore, discussed later in this paper. In their seminal article, Chin and Benne (1961) articulate three different strategies of planned goal-oriented change often employed in organizations — the empirical-rationale strategy, the power-coercive strategy and the normative reeducative strategy (for a summary see Pochron, 2008). The normative-reeducative strategy most closely aligns with the principles of stakeholder engagement. An underlying assumption of this change strategy is that individuals 'must participate in [their] own re-education if [they are] to be re-educated at all' (Chin & Benne, 1961, p. 32). Chin and Benne argue people are motivated to take an active participative role in the planning and implementation of organization change in order to satisfy inherent personal needs. This participative process requires authentic communication and dialogue between leaders and the organizational members to build consensus, resolve conflicts and address resistance or ambivalence (Bridges, 1991; Bruckman, 2008; Szabla, 2007). In an empirical study of employees facing a change in their human resource appraisal system, Szabla (2007) found that employees who had a participative role (consistent with a normative-reeducative change strategy) were 'optimistic, delighted and energized . . . they experienced the most positive beliefs, the most positive emotions, and had the highest intentions to support the change' (p. 550).

Support for an employee participative role in change processes (based on the normative-reeducative strategy) can be found in the Quinn, Spreitzer, and Brown (2000) Advanced Change Theory (ACT) model, which articulates specific principles of participant engagement as follows:

- recognize hypocrisy and patterns of self-deception;
- create personal change through value clarification and alignment of behaviours;
- free oneself from the system of external sanctions;
- develop a vision for the common good;
- take action to the edge of chaos;
- maintain reverence for others involved in change;
- inspire others to enact their best selves;
- model counterintuitive, paradoxical behaviour; and
- change self and system.

The normative-reeducative strategy is explicitly or implicitly utilized in many models of organizational development (for a summary, see Szabla, 2007) and can be referenced here in terms of the behaviours and attitudes that require strengthening as part of the early change process. Strengthening is what Lewin (1952) describes as 'unfreezing' for change. Such early strengthening is also urged in Burke's (2008) prelaunch phase requiring leader self-awareness and holding motives and values that are consistent with the change goals. Unfreezing and prelaunch type change processes align with readiness for change.

Literature on readiness for change by authors such as Armenakis and Harris (2009) Kotter (2007, 2012), and I. Smith (2006) point to factors such as building excitement, a sense of need and urgency, a plan of action, vision and direction, effective communication, and leadership to be achieved through partnership, coalition and genuine involvement of organizational members. Armenakis and Harris (2009) tie most of these issues together under the following five overarching 'readiness to change' beliefs that impact an employee's motivation for change:

> (a) discrepancy; (b) appropriateness; (c) efficacy; (d) principal support; and (e) valence. . . . *Discrepancy* refers to the belief that a change is needed; that there is a significant gap between the current state of the organization and what it should be. *Appropriateness* reflects the belief that a specific change designed to address a discrepancy is the correct one for the situation. *Efficacy* refers to the belief that the change recipient and the organization can successfully implement a change. *Principal support* is the belief that the formal leaders (vertical change agents) in an organization are committed to the success of a change and that it is not going to be another passing fad or program of the month. Furthermore, we include as principals the opinion leaders who can serve as horizontal change agents. Finally, *valence* reflects the belief that the change is beneficial to the change recipient; there is something of benefit in it for them. (Armenakis & Harris, 2009, p. 129)

Armenakis and Harris (2009) describe a number of processes that contribute to these changes in employee attitudes: effective organizational diagnosis; sending out change messages that directly address beliefs about the urgency, importance and efficacy of the change; and active participation (consistent with the normative-reeducative change strategy). Armenakis and

Harris further note that 'persuasive communication may not be as effective as active participation' (p. 135). While Armenakis and Harris refer to these processes as 'sensitiz[ing those affected by the change] to the possibility of an impending organizational change' (p. 130), they do not feel these processes are sufficient to produce organizational change itself.

Other authors are explicit in suggesting that organizational change must begin with the active participation of key organizational stakeholders throughout all levels (beyond the executive level) in shared decision-making about the change goals, removal of obstacles and resistance, and initiation of sustainable action (Appelbaum & Wohl, 2000; Bushe & Marshak, 2009). Appelbaum and Wohl (2000) argue these activities result in new learning that generates dissatisfaction with the status quo, strong attraction to move towards a new state and appeal for a well thought out strategy. These authors state that managers who engage in early stage learning processes about the change strategy generate greater trust, exhibit better role model behaviour and are better communicators with other levels of employees who are involved in or affected by the change process.

While a strong body of literature supports the notion of a need for active participation of organizational members in planning and implementing change, there is an absence of clarity on what these processes of participation should be. One can argue that action research promotes engagement of key stakeholders throughout many levels of an organization and that heightened engagement contributes to enhanced organizational readiness for change. The following discussion of stakeholder engagement should clarify its potential in initiating and sustaining change initiatives.

Engagement

Employee engagement is often characterized as a state with energy, involvement, efficacy and connection with work activities (Saks, 2006; Schaufeli, Salanova, González-Romá,

& Bakker, 2002). Schaufeli et al. (2002) further define engagement as 'a positive, fulfilling, work-related state of mind that is characterized by vigor, dedication, and absorption' (p. 74). According to the positive psychology theorists, engaged employees have positive emotions and attitudes of hope, optimism, efficacy, and resilience — what has been termed their *positive psychological capital*, PsyCap for short (see Luthans, Avolio, Avey, & Norman, 2007). Avey, Wernsing, and Luthans (2008) explored the relationship between employee engagement and attitudes toward organizational change in an empirical study with 132 mostly nonmanagerial employees. They concluded that 'employees' positive resources are associated with desired attitudes (emotional engagement) and behaviors (organizational citizenship) that previous research has shown to directly and indirectly facilitate and enhance positive organizational change' (p. 64).

Kahn (1990) described three psychological conditions as antecedents to engagement: psychological meaningfulness, safety and availability. In the change context, meaningfulness is considered to be *derived from* one's participation in the change process, but that a sense of availability and safety needs to be *created* in order for full engagement to occur (Gruman & Saks, 2011). In other words, employees who feel their work is meaningful derive satisfaction that their actions are related to a larger and more enduring purpose or end. Psychological safety refers to the belief or feeling that there are no undesirable or negative consequences from those actions. Availability refers to having access to the necessary resources—in the case of change initiatives, this means having both information and decision makers at the table. Psychological safety and availability will be focussed on in more detail later to show how they contribute to the early engagement phases of change initiatives.

Involving or engaging stakeholders early in a change initiative can result in them feeling more positive, connected and dedicated, having a greater sense of ownership, and consequently being less resistant to the change process (Szabla, 2007). Other advantages of early engagement in a change process include: increased understanding of each stakeholder's part in the bigger picture; enhanced focus on finding solutions based on this bigger picture vision; and greater stakeholder understanding of how their 'actions may influence the whole system' (Scharmer, 2009, p. 217).

Bunker and Alban (2006) propose that knowing who needs to be part of the conversation, valuing each voice and establishing collaborative ground are important considerations for effective engagement. All three of these elements significantly contribute to higher levels of stakeholder availability and involvement in work activities. These are all relational elements and, as M. L. Smith (2006) states:

> It is the nature of the web of relationships that exists among all of the individuals to whom we are connected that is likely to have a profound influence on our efforts to engage in a process of individual (and intentional) change. (p. 719)

Engaged employees experience meaningfulness in their work activities (Kahn, 1990). Employees who participate in dialogue and deliberation to share perspectives about a change initiative experience deeper engagement and, therefore, are more open to accept other points of view, change their own understanding, form new ideas and solutions and adopt new practices related to the change initiative. Raelin (2012) supports this notion, arguing that 'people join a dialogue provided they are interested in listening to one, in reflecting upon perspectives different from their own and in entertaining the prospect of being changed by what they learn' (p. 8). Raelin goes on to describe deliberation for the purposes of decision making as an output of the dialogic process, characterizing 'dialogue and deliberation as a collaborative form of discourse in which wisdom is sought not just through one's eyes but through others' (pp. 8–9). Consistent with these ideas, Bushe (2012) has articulated a dialogic organizational development theory of practice that involves use of group inquiry and dialogic methods or events such as Open Space, Appreciative Inquiry Summits and hosted conversations to work through change goals, challenges and ideas. Bushe stated, 'The point of these events . . . is to unearth, catalyze and support the multitude of motivations and ideas that already exist in the organization, in the service of the change goal' (p. 4). Bushe firmly believes that transformational change requires thinking about possibilities and that this is facilitated through generative conversations, which invite people to focus on the future they want to create together.

These perspectives on dialogue, deliberation and opening oneself to new ways of seeing and thinking, involve complex processes that are absent from many descriptions of organizational change initiatives. Adopting a stance that values new points of view and paradigms and encourages participation in authentic collaborative dialogue belies a great deal of relational complexity (Piggot-Irvine, 2012). Essentially, such a stance is nondefensive; it involves adopting strategies and values that are both noncontrolling and nonavoiding when difficult issues need to be discussed. In the early stages of change, difficult issues often arise, but if nondefensive dialogue is practised, the issues are usually resolved and higher levels of trust result. Trust creates an accepting space for generation of new ideas as well as workplace engagement and thriving (Albrecht & Hall, 1991; Carmeli & Spreitzer, 2009).

In summary, many organizational change models would benefit from a greater emphasis on a dialogic engagement phase with stakeholders at multiple levels in the organization. The following section discusses how these engagement principles are articulated through the application of action research as a methodology of collaborative inquiry, reflection, and action. Action research is discussed more generally and its application in the early phases of specific organizational change initiatives is described.

General Principles of Action Research as an Inquiry and Change Methodology

Action research is a loose term covering a variety of approaches for social research within organizations and other social systems. The origins of action research can be found in the works of Lewin (1946, 1952), Kolb (1984), and Carr and Kemmis (1986), but many others have contributed to the field (see Zuber-Skerritt, 2012, for a summary). Reason and Bradbury (2001) provide the following widely cited definition of action research:

> Action research is a participatory, democratic process concerned with developing practical knowledge in the pursuit of worthwhile human purposes, grounded in a participatory worldview . . . it seeks to bring together action and reflection, theory and practice, in participation with others, in the pursuit of practical solutions to issues of pressing concern. (p. 1)

The second component of this definition is not too far removed from that posed by Sankaran, Tay, and Orr (2009) who describe action research as 'a process of collaborative enquiry carried out by people affected by a problem or concern, often using a cyclical process to increase their understanding of the real problem before moving towards a solution' (p. 181). Both Reason and Bradbury and Sankaran et al. define action research within a problem-solving framework focussed on organizational improvement and the analysis of specifically identified organizational challenges (as do Coghlan & Brannick, 2010; Dick, 2001; Kemmis & McTaggart, 1995; Piggot-Irvine et al., 2011; Preskill & Torres, 1999; Zuber-Skerritt, 2002; and many others).

Coghlan and Brannick (2010) and Stringer (2007) strongly support the application of rigorous data collection methodologies within action research and assert that interpretation and conceptualization are necessary stages that contribute to understanding (Grubbs, 2001) and causal explanation (Aguinis, 1993). Theoretical explanations may both inform (e.g., a literature review pre-activity to data collection) or be derived from the data (theory emergent from the data). As Checkland (1991) and Dickens and Watkins (1999) suggest, this type of informed data collection activity is then used to guide organizational action or practice.

Most authors define action research as series of cycles that contain Lewin's (1952) 'moments' in which researchers plan (problem and situation analysis — sometimes also called reconnaissance), act (implementation of a plan for improvement), observe (evaluation of the improvements) and reflect (on all of the moments as well as the overall process and outcomes). Invariably, new cycles emerge from the reflection and for this reason action research is often described as iterative.

This paper focuses on the first phases of activity in which members of the organization are engaged in preparing for the change initiative. Stringer (2007) recognizes that one cannot act or take action in an organization or community without preliminary stages that involve participants collaboratively building an understanding of the context and thinking (reflecting) to determine what action steps to take. Stringer sees action research as a 'collaborative approach to investigation that seeks to engage "subjects" as equal and full participants in the research process' (p. 10). Coghlan and Brannick (2010) also highlight the importance of engagement by establishing a 'constructing' stage in which dialogue occurs with the project's stakeholders. This stage involves 'constructing the initiative with significant stakeholders and systematically generating and collecting research data about an ongoing system relative to some objective or need' (p. 64). Coghlan and Brannick also recognize the importance of engagement throughout the change implementation process but do not articulate a specific mechanism by which this is accomplished.

This stage of 'constructing the context' (Coghlan & Brannick, 2010) or 'planning' the action intervention (Zuber-Skerrit, 2012) involves engagement of individuals and groups who are key stakeholders to the change. This stage is seen as a foundational condition for organizational change readiness and is described in detail in the Action Research Engagement Model (ARE) section below. The ARE model seeks to explicate an action research cycle of collaborative inquiry, dialogue, reflection and deliberation that strengthens the readiness of the organization to launch a structural or process change intervention. What is distinctive about the ARE model is what it adds to organizational change models as well action research models through its focus on an oft underemphasized foundation in which researchers engage and create new motivation and learning among a broad sector of organizational stakeholders about the desired change, reframe their views in relation to what they learn from others, enhance their understanding of what needs to change through situation analysis, and set direction for the change through visioning and strategic planning.

The Action Research Engagement Model

The ARE model focuses on the planning, preparatory or context setting, stages of action research. In the planning stage, key organizational members engage with each other in inquiry, collaborative dialogue and deliberation to ask questions; gather organizational data; conduct systematic data analysis; reflect on what the data means; and deliberate on change options and future action. The ARE model is associated with shifting attitudes, perspectives, knowledge and values among people in the organization by enhancing meaningfulness, clarity and commonality of purpose, motivation, and commitment for change. Additionally, the ARE model clarifies the need, direction and strategies for change, resulting in the development of an organizational change action plan. Figure 1 provides an illustration of the ARE model and shows its connection to the later traditional stages of action implementation.

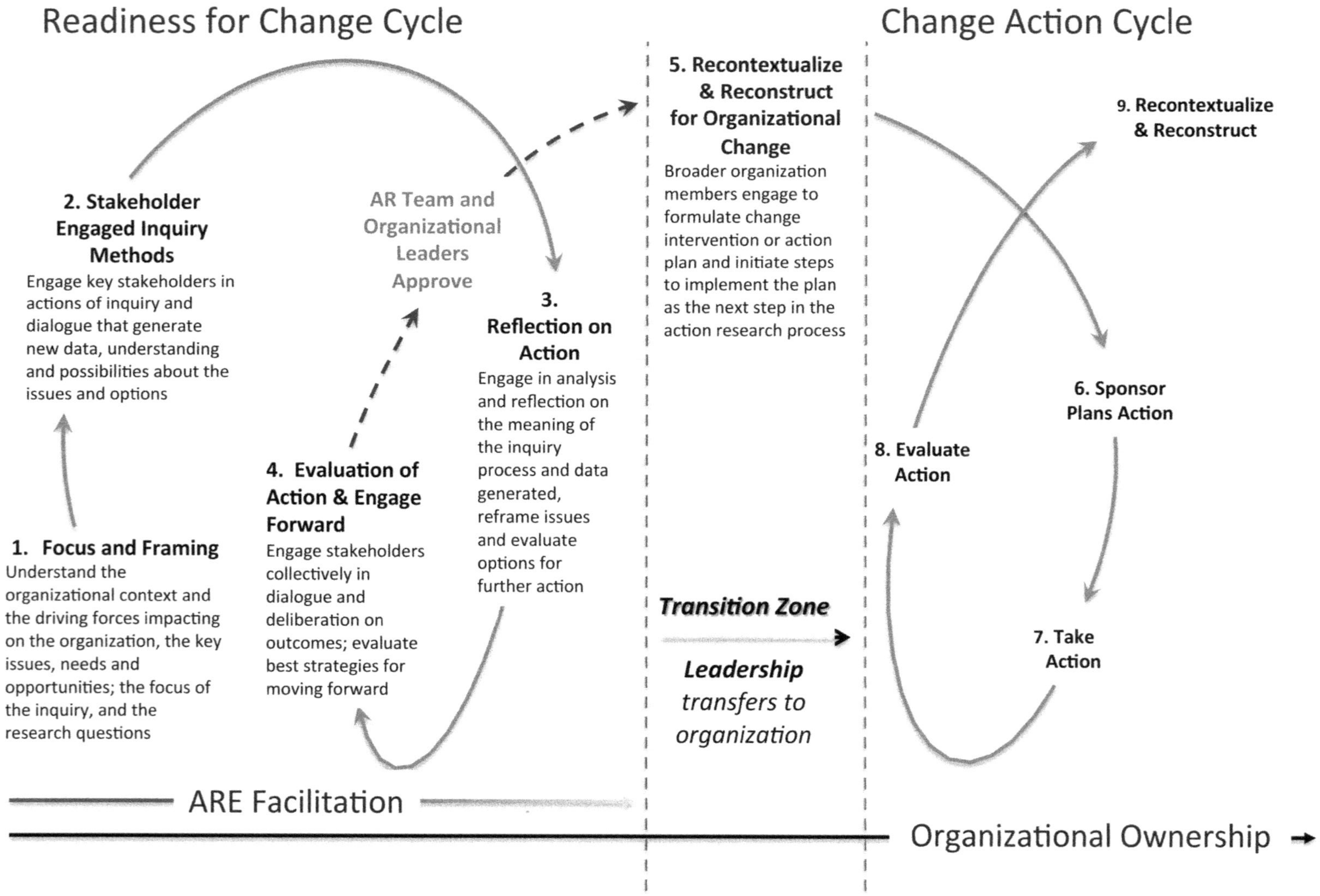

Readiness for Change Cycle

Change Action Cycle

2. Stakeholder Engaged Inquiry Methods
Engage key stakeholders in actions of inquiry and dialogue that generate new data, understanding and possibilities about the issues and options

AR Team and Organizational Leaders Approve

3. Reflection on Action
Engage in analysis and reflection on the meaning of the inquiry process and data generated, reframe issues and evaluate options for further action

1. Focus and Framing
Understand the organizational context and the driving forces impacting on the organization, the key issues, needs and opportunities; the focus of the inquiry, and the research questions

4. Evaluation of Action & Engage Forward
Engage stakeholders collectively in dialogue and deliberation on outcomes; evaluate best strategies for moving forward

5. Recontextualize & Reconstruct for Organizational Change
Broader organization members engage to formulate change intervention or action plan and initiate steps to implement the plan as the next step in the action research process

Transition Zone

Leadership *transfers to organization*

9. Recontextualize & Reconstruct

6. Sponsor Plans Action

8. Evaluate Action

7. Take Action

ARE Facilitation

Organizational Ownership →

Figure 1. The action research engagement model. Modified version of the original organizational action research (OAR) model (Rowe, Agger-Gupta, Harris, & Graf, 2011).

Note. AR = Action Research; ARE = Action Research Engagement.

The following stages of action research are embedded in the ARE model:

1. Focus and Framing is the stage in which researchers carry out a situation analysis to understand the organizational context, recognize the driving forces impacting the organization, and identify the key issues and focus of the inquiry. Literature is explored and research questions are formulated.
2. Stakeholder Engaged Inquiry Methods are used to engage key stakeholders in actions of inquiry, data gathering and dialogue that generate new information and ideas, greater understanding of the issues, and explore options that are shared across stakeholders and within the organization.
3. Reflection on Action is the stage in which researchers engage in analysis and reflection on the inquiry process and data generated. Issues are reframed, deriving deeper meaning, and evaluation of the strength of options for further action occurs.
4. Evaluation of Action and Engage Forward is the step in which stakeholders collectively engage in dialogue and deliberate on outcomes of the action inquiry, evaluating best strategies and actions for moving forward.
5. Recontextualize and Reconstruct for Organizational Change occurs at the organization level, formulating a senior-level endorsed change intervention or action plan to initiate steps to implement the plan as the next step in the action research process.

Table 2 provides a summary of changes among the participants in areas of new knowledge, perspectives and attitudes at each of the stages or moments of the ARE model. Each of the ARE stages is more fully described in the following sections.

Table 2. *Action Research Cycle Stages and Outcomes*

Stages of the ARE Process	Participants' new perspectives and attitudes	Participants' new behaviours, processes or structures	Participants' new knowledge
Focus and Framing	Shared belief in the need for change, its goals and the organization's capacity to be successful.	Reads and/or discusses the content of background materials; agrees to participate in the inquiry and a dialogic event.	A clearly identified need for inquiry and direction for change promoted by organizational leaders and key stakeholders. Shared interpretation of drivers for change.
Stakeholder Engaged Inquiry Methods	Willingness to consider other points of view in relation to one's own, to arrive at different perspectives. Open to alternatives to status quo.	Managers, employees and other stakeholders participate in inquiry activities, including dialogic group events with other stakeholders at any levels. Listen to other points of view. New communicative relations formed among participants.	A shared understanding of issues and options identified by key stakeholders in the organization. New knowledge about roles and perspective of diverse others in organization.
Reflection on Action	Open to new interpretations and working relationships; openness to doing things differently.	Skills in dialogic engagement; skills in reflection and analysis; new relational communication skills.	New knowledge of findings and conclusions related to the research questions and of options/recommendations for new practices, structural and processes changes. Shared understanding of drivers of change and strategies.
Evaluation of Action and Engage Forward	Perceived urgency for change; strategies for moving forward are viewed as viable and feasible, by most, if not all, stakeholders.	Expanded working relationships and dialogic processes established for future groups. Expanded circle of stakeholders involved in the change initiative. Stakeholders are excited and motivated to embrace change.	Proposed change strategy is redefined and/or modified, validated and accepted and endorsed by key organizational leaders as important and requiring attention.
Recontextualize and Reconstruct for Organizational Change	Belief in and commitment to the change goals and processes across key areas of the organization.	Organizations take ownership of the change strategy and proposed plan. Key messages on the intervention plan are disseminated; feedback sought and incorporated into the plan.	The intervention plan is understood and endorsed by all levels of the entire organization.

Stage 1: The focus and framing. The purpose of this stage in the ARE is to carry out a situation analysis to understand the organizational context and the driving forces impacting on the organization and to identify the key issues and focus of the inquiry. Most ARE projects begin with a topic of concern — something that is happening in the organization that warrants attention, perhaps something of great urgency. This might be a new or more strongly stated directive from senior leadership or the board, a serious problem or issue impacting on the performance of the organization in some area, or an opportunity to implement a new initiative.

It is essential that the focus and framing stage of the project generates a full understanding of the background, or precipitating context, related to the topic of concern. Effort should be taken to understand why the topic is significant to the organization, what factors impact the organization and contribute to this topic of concern, and who is or will be impacted by this topic of concern. The organizational system is explored, including the mission, goals, values and culture of the organization as it relates to the issue. A champion or lead investigator volunteers or is assigned to take on the initiative. This could be a manager or another senior leader in the organization, a university researcher, or an external consultant.

The first step in this stage is to form an Inquiry Team who will coordinate and lead the ARE project. This team typically includes the lead investigator plus one to three key representatives from the organization. This team accepts responsibility to implement the ARE project, guide the processes, convene meetings, ensure data are gathered and compiled and facilitate decision making. Information is gathered through the following processes, including but not limited to:

- interviews with key organizational stakeholders to identify problems, challenges, issues, and opportunities;
- a review of organizational documents on mission, vision, values and performance;

- analysis of archival reports that provide more empirical data on the topic of concern;
- a literature review on relevant areas of the topic and why it should be important to the organization;
- analysis of the organizational systems and structure underpinning the context of the change;
- the determination of which key stakeholders should be further involved; and
- the determination of appropriate, strategic, and specific methods for further stakeholder engagement in the next stage of the ARE model.

There are four key outputs at the conclusion of the focus and framing stage of the ARE model:

1. Statement of the overarching, key, research question, which includes reference to what is to change and in what area (department or unit) of the organization.
2. Articulation of the inquiry subquestions, which relate to specific desired learning goals or outputs of each phase of the project.
3. An assessment of whether success is likely and a pilot project possible.
4. A plan for a manageably-scoped sequence of inquiry methods appropriate for the inquiry subquestions.

Stage 2: Stakeholder engaged inquiry methods. During this stage, key stakeholders participate in a variety of inquiry activities to learn more about the issues to generate data related to the research questions, explore different perspectives related to the issues and generate new ideas and strategies or action plans to resolve the problem or take advantage of new opportunity. Participants engage in a variety of inquiry and questioning activities during this stage that may include the use of surveys and interviews to obtain individual opinions, perspectives, experiences, and knowledge related to the topic of concern, but will normally include a group dialogic process among key stakeholders to share these perspectives with others.

A group dialogic process might be a large group method for 20–100 diverse individuals such as a world café (Brown & Isaacs, 2005), appreciative inquiry summit (Ludema, Whitney, Mohr, & Griffin, 2003), future search (Weisbord & Janoff, 2000), matrix interviews (National Managers' Community, 2002) and open space technology (Owen, 1997). A smaller group process, such as a focus group (Krueger & Casey, 2009) or learning circles (Wade & Hammick, 1999) might be more suitable for groups of 5–10 homogeneous individuals who are focussed on understanding a problem, evaluating strategies or making decisions. For a review of these group methods, and how they can be used to generate data while engaging participants in dialogue and inquiry for the purposes of systemic change, see Bunker and Alban (2006).

The use of multiple methods with diverse participant groups creates opportunity to triangulate the different perspectives and findings to derive intersecting or common themes across the different settings. Additionally, the use of quantitative tools (e.g., a survey with rating or check list questions) in combination with qualitative tools (i.e., any tool that generates text and open ended participants opinions) can be used strategically to balance classifying an issue with exploration in a mixed method approaches (Creswell, 2009; Creswell & Plano Clark, 2007). Creswell (2009) provides a comprehensive description of a mixed method approach, in which different quantitative and qualitative tools are combined to identify the extent and nature of an organizational opportunity, problem or issue, explore its significance and meaning to others, and explore ideas for next steps.

When key organizational stakeholders engage as a group in discourse about the topic of concern, they are exposed to different perspectives on the issue, can reframe their own perspectives, collectively generate new and innovative solutions to challenging issues and develop the new relationships and trust needed to sustain implementation of new ideas. The outcomes of this phase fall into three categories:

1. New data on the topic of concern, related to the nature and significance of the opportunities, challenge, problem or issues across different sectors or levels of the organization, which include how potential changes in the organization will impact on the organizational members and/or its customers and external stakeholders.
2. New ideas on strategies and processes to implement on how to resolve or solve the organizational issue or problem, or how to take advantage of an opportunity.
3. New relational skills and connections among the participants (e.g., awareness of different perspectives, ability to listen and communicate, respect and collaborative intentions, etc.).

Stage 3: Reflection on action. The purpose of this stage is to engage key stakeholders in a process to make meaning of the data gathered in the previous stage, to identify overarching themes and subthemes, and to assess the implications of what is being learnt. The meaning-making process often starts while the data are first being collected, especially when data are generated during group dialogue. As perspectives, experiences and knowledge are shared, participants intuitively begin to organize what they are hearing into themes; these themes often feed back into the dialogue as further questions for consideration. The intuitive and preliminary meaning-making process transitions into formal data analysis. Since there may be both quantitative survey data as well as textual data from the discussion forums, a variety of analytical tools may be employed. Data typically are compiled, sorted and mapped into themes and subthemes, ensuring there is always evidence to support conclusions that are being offered. All themes and subthemes are critically evaluated for whether they are sustainable and representative of the data generated during the Engaged Inquiry phase. Conclusions may be further verified with key stakeholders by having individuals participate in the analysis process, read the summary reports or participate in a presentation of findings. A reflection phase may cycle back into a renewed inquiry phase.

The output of this stage is generally a report on findings and key conclusions from the engaged inquiry phase. This report should detail all inquiry processes, outline who was involved, offer the basis for the theming of findings, and indicate how conclusions were derived. Literature is used to validate the conclusions and provide further explanation on the meaning of the findings, especially in relation to the organizational change goals.

Stage 4: Evaluation of action and engage forward. This stage involves a group of decision makers engaged in further dialogue and deliberation on the outcomes of ARE Stage 3, evaluating best strategies and actions for moving forward with the change initiative. This deliberative process entails assessing the strengths and weaknesses of the recommended strategies and future actions in terms of their urgency, importance, feasibility and appropriateness. Resources and timelines are considered. Many ideas may be relegated to low priority value due to difficulty or cost of implementation. Typically, one or more meetings are held, perhaps framed as a focus group or some other decision-making process. The output of this process is an approved set of recommendations and an action plan that will go forward to senior leadership or the governing body.

Stage 5: Recontextualize and reconstruct for organizational change. Following the development of recommendations, the change initiative transitions to the organizational department or unit responsible for implementing the recommendations. At this stage of the ARE process, new stakeholders may be engaged to assist in the translation of the recommendations into specific intervention action plans and to carry out their implementation. It is at this stage that progress may stall. The expanded or new implementation team or department may need to go through their own process of engagement (inquiry, dialogue, reflection and deliberation) to embrace the findings and recommendations previously generated.

The greater the degree that key stakeholders in the previous phases act as communicators to bridge with the implementation team or department, the greater the likelihood that the change effort will continue. The message of change and its significance should be disseminated throughout the organization, with opportunities created for further questions and participation in the implementation of the change strategies.

The intended outcome from this stage is a sustained change initiative with specific strategies and actions implemented. Structural or process changes may occur in the organization or new programmes may be implemented. Next steps involve evaluation of these changes to determine the success of the initiative with respect to the original or emerging challenge, opportunity, problem or issues.

ARE Model Case Studies

The following two case studies provide examples of how the ARE model was used in organizational change projects. The examples are drawn from student capstone projects from a university graduate-level leadership programme. Projects have been undertaken by working professionals, typically in their organizations, as part of the Master of Arts degree.

ARE Case I. An excellent example of the ARE model can be seen in Blakley's (2012) project to support the implementation of lean management practices in a health region in Canada. Blakley describes lean management as processes that reduce waste so as to increase value to customer (Ballé & Ballé, 2009; Sassenberg, 2008), as well as being a philosophy of continuous improvement in which leaders are engaging staff and 'out there connecting dots, sharing the vision' (Kenney, 2011, p. 181).

Blakley's overarching question was: 'How can the leadership community within the Saskatoon Health Region build on its leadership strengths in support of the new lean management system?' (p. 9). Blakley defined the following subquestions to assist in understanding the leadership capacity within the region's leadership community:

1. What are the current leadership strengths, within leadership community, that will contribute to leading in a lean management system?
2. What are the leadership challenges, within leadership community, that will be encountered as they move to support a new lean management system?
3. What does the leadership community need to lead in a lean management system? (p. 9)

As part of the focus and framing (ARE Stage 1), there was a call within the health region for changing leadership perspectives and practices to support a new lean management system that would improve the quality and safety of care across the region while bringing costs into line. The health region was challenged to find 'efficiencies in the system while increasing the quality and safety of the care provided' (Blakley, 2012, p. 13). The organization embarked on a reorganization 'committed to a lean management system, a much more rigorous commitment to quality and safety requiring a philosophical change in how things are done in the organization' (Blakley, 2012, p. 20). An extensive review of the literature was carried out to identify leadership behaviours that supported the implementation of lean strategies/practices as well as the usual barriers and challenges. 'Lean can be seen as having both a philosophical as well as a practical orientation' (Blakley, 2012, p. 17).

While the literature search helped inform the inquiry team, it did not create the conditions for change across the key stakeholders in the system. Consequently, the next step was to implement an action research methodology to engage action (ARE Stage 2) with key stakeholders 'to reflect on and gain new insights . . . analyze the situation correctly, consider findings, identify all the possible alternative solutions, and plan how to keep what is working and change what is not' (Blakley, 2012, p. 34). All members of the leadership community (nine vice-presidents, 14 physician dyad leaders, and 43 directors) were invited to a series of learning circles and later to a world café. The three learning circles involved 15 individuals, two groups consisting of combinations of vice-presidents and physician leaders and one circle for directors (Blakley, 2012). A two-part world café included directors in the first part and vice-presidents and dyad physician leaders in the second part. 'In total 21 participants took part in the world café, which constituted approximately 24% of [the region's] leadership community' (Blakley, 2012, p. 36). Overall, 41% of leadership community members attended at least one of the learning circles or the world café event. According to the facilitator,

> The world café event focussed on concrete ideas to build on the region's leadership strengths, support leaders in their growth and development as lean leaders, and challenge the underlying and often unwritten rules and assumptions that might limit leader's ability to effectively build and sustain a lean management system. (Blakley, 2012, p. 46)

Through data analysis and reflection (ARE Stage 3), Blakley's (2012) findings revealed that lean management systems require new leadership behaviours that include a strong coaching and teamwork focus. Blakley's findings also identified the need for a strong coalition with physicians to sustain the change and highlighted key aspects of transformational change, the excitement of being involved in the transformation, the desire to actively engage in all aspects of the transformation, the potential of leadership fatigue and the potential negative impacts of the change action on teamwork and relationships. Blakley reviewed the significant findings from this ARE process with the sponsor and leadership team (ARE Stage 3), to 'vet proposed actions, which had evolved as a result of the findings and literature reviewed' (p. 85). Blakley noted that she 'regularly engaged [her] sponsor either in person or online . . . provided her with advance copies of all chapters [of the final report] ensuring she had an opportunity to provide input' (p. 86). By capturing the essence of the ARE model (ARE Stages 4 and 5), successful adoption of the inquiry recommendations into the organization was achieved by engaging additional leadership team members who 'would have a direct or indirect role in assisting the organization in implementing the recommendations' (Blakley, 2012, p. 85).

Blakley (2012), the principle investigator in this case study, reported that progress had already begun as a result of this project (ARE Stage 5). Following the research, project meetings occurred to present the recommendations to health region senior leadership team, the staff of the regional Kaizen Promotion Office (KPO), and the provincial Joint Workforce Planning Committee (JWPC) made up of Vice Presidents of Human Resources from across the province. Based on a robust discussion at the JWPC following the research presentation, the committee struck a small working group to consider Blakley's recommendations and to bring back a brief action plan on how to collectively tackle a small number of the recommendations over the next year (ARE Stage 6).

Implementation of Blakley's (2012) action research project recommendations has begun at a rapid pace (ARE Stage 6 and ARE Stage 7) within the organization. Based on the research it became evident that work needed to begin immediately to build coaching modules into the workplace. The province's new health system leadership and succession programme was created around the health competency framework and structured to support the new lean management system. Coaching has now been included as a central element to its 18-month programme. The recommendation to clearly articulate lean leader behaviours also received immediate interest and reaction when the research was presented. As a result, the organization is working to clearly articulate what these behaviours are and include them in the interview guides and performance appraisals (Blakley, 2012). The final recommendation in the action research report that highlighted the need to bridge the gap between the 1-day Kaizen basic training and the 56-day lean leader certification is underway (Blakley, 2012). The research reinforced what many in the KPO had already identified as a barrier and work is now underway locally and provincially to create and offer value stream mapping modules in the organization's fiscal year 2013–2014.

What is notable about this ARE project is the emergence of meaningful findings and recommendations that have assisted the health region in developing more effective leadership practices to support the lean management strategy. Blakley (2012) reported that stakeholders were more 'excited and willing to lead the changes required to implement the new lean management system' (p. 75) and more willing to work in teams to accomplish goals and provide or receive coaching to facilitate operational goals (ARE Stage 7).

ARE Case 2. Robertson's (2012) project adopted the ARE model to improve the delivery of customer service in a small city of 80,000 in western Canada. The overarching question was: "What employee engagement initiatives can the Development and Engineering Services department at the [city name] undertake to improve customer service?" (Robertson, 2012, p. 2). Subquestions were designed to inform the department on employee engagement and customer service improvement: "1. How does employee engagement impact customer service? 2. How can [department] employees engage in improving customer service? 3. What organizational or system support do Development and Engineering employees need to improve customer service?" (p. 2).

In the initial stages of focus and framing (ARE Stage 1), the department identified the need to enhance employee engagement initiatives with an intended result of 'improved citizen satisfaction with customer service' (Robertson, 2012, p. 1). Since 2003, the city had experienced declining customer satisfaction ratings. Although efforts had been placed on reigniting the city's More Value Promise (MVP) customer service programme (Robertson, 2012), customer satisfaction levels had continued to decline. The focus and framing also uncovered staff's general apathy for and lack of interest in the MVP or similar customer service programmes. The city administration acts as the governing body providing services and amenities to all residents in the city and is fully funded through taxes, fees, and government grants (Robertson, 2012). Customer service satisfaction can positively or severely impact on the city's service delivery model.

A significant review of the literature was conducted to 'understand how customer service improvements can be achieved at [the city]' (Robertson, 2012, p. 11) through exploring employee engagement and customer services best practices. Robertson's (2012) review of the literature also explored key elements that could promote organizational change success for the city as they embarked on enhancing employee engagement to improve customer service.

An action research methodology was used to engage action (ARE Stage 2) that enabled key stakeholders 'to collaboratively find effective solutions to everyday customer service delivery challenges' (Robertson, 2012, p. 21). All 24 staff in one operational city department, whose primary focus was customer service, were invited to participate in an interview matrix. The 16 participants who attended the interview matrix 'had an opportunity to engage their colleagues in the customer services issue by asking questions of one another' (Robertson, 2012, p. 25) that appeared to 'foster trust and openness while facilitating organizational learning during the dialogue' (p. 26). Following the interview matrix, all six senior management team members were invited to attend a focus group to share their views and perspectives on customer service and employee engagement within the city. Through answering the probing questions, the five focus group participants 'clarified and elicited deeper information on customer service strengths and weakness within the [city]' (Robertson, 2012, p. 29). Engagement was high as evidenced by the fact that a total of 67% of the customer service staff in one department and 90% of the senior management team for the whole organization participated in this research project (Robertson, 2012). In addition to the interview matrix and interviews, Robertson (2012) conducted a document review of 'publically available documentation relevant to the [study]' (p. 25).

The next step in Robertson's (2012) project (ARE Stage 3) involved data analysis and reflection. Key findings exposed elements of successful customer service delivery for the city. The findings uncovered the employee's quest for more empowerment within the workplace to improve customer service.. Positive employee recognition and respect from the client appeared to be a key motivational factor 'to provide better service' (Robertson, 2012, p. 39). The findings also showed the senior management's team's need to 'foster increased employee recognition' (Robertson, 2012, p. 39) and highlighted the importance of strong leadership to build and sustain the organization's commitment to customer service. Robertson presented seven recommendations to the sponsoring organization that encompassed improving customer service through optimizing employee engagement.

Consultation with the sponsor and key stakeholders (ARE Stages 4 and 5) incorporated a strong collaborative lens, one that embraced the ARE model of inclusiveness, stakeholder engagement, and ownership of the recommendations. The project recommendations signified 'the most important component to customer service improvement is understanding customer needs and developing service delivery to meet them' (Robertson, 2012, p. 77) and provided a foundation for the city to consider as they strive to 'increase employee connection and commitment to the City's purpose' (p. 77). Robertson (2012) presented a synopsis of the research project, findings, and recommendations to the department, senior management team and the mayor of the city. The organization underwent a personality assessment team-building exercise to begin the process and shifts required to implement the recommendations (ARE Stages 6 and 7). Staff's interest in the project was evidenced through their request for a presentation at the completion of the project (Robertson, 2012).

Adopting the ARE model presented an opportunity for the city to engage staff and senior management to explore opportunities that can strengthen customer service delivery. Key stakeholders gained a greater understanding of the city's goals and the role they play in supporting the city to achieve these goals. In ARE Stage 7, Robertson's (2012) project sponsor noted his commitment to implementing the recommendations and ensuring staff understood the value of their participation in this project: 'He would like them to be aware of how their input was put to use and how it may influence customer service improvements' (Robertson, 2012, p. 78).

Conclusion

The ARE projects described in the preceding section help to illustrate the key principles and processes of the ARE model, including:

1. Identification of a significant issue or opportunity for the organization in which change or growth is intended.
2. A project goal (stated as a research question) that seeks learning, inquiry and specific change in a designated unit or among a group of people.
3. Organizational sponsorship (co-ownership) in an inquiry action change process.
4. Systems analysis of the organizational context and factors underlying the identified issues.
5. Identification of key stakeholders who would be impacted by and are, therefore, important contributors to the success of the intended change.
6. Engagement of key stakeholders in a cyclical process of focusing and framing of the issues, engaging action and data collection about the issue and strategies for change, reflecting and meaning making, engaging a broader community in moving forward, and recontextualizing and reconstructing ongoing organizational change.

What is significant about the ARE process are the deliberate steps to engage key organizational stakeholders in cyclical processes of inquiry, reflection and action that fundamentally seeks to change stakeholders' perspectives and paradigms about the issues at hand, foster interest and motivation and create a climate of commitment to move forward in a collaborative manner and implement organizational change. These processes create the conditions for members of an organization, beginning with key stakeholders, to: get 'ready for change' and become motivated and committed to change because they have arrived at a common understanding of the issues; to develop new beliefs, insights, and perspectives on why and wherefores; and, to have established new partnerships and networks for moving action forward. These processes also create the potential for transformational change (Anderson & Ackerman Anderson, 2001; Torbert, 2004), in which individuals and groups reframe beliefs and perspectives and change occurs in the fundamental nature of the organization.

Stakeholder engagement is not passive observation nor participation by 'name only' on committees or task groups, but rather an active process of inquiry and collaborative dialogue, structured around research questions, that puts existing practices and operations into question and organizes leaders and stakeholders to implement change actions. ARE fosters an effective and engaging organizational change process.

References

Aguinis, H. (1993). Action research and scientific method: Presumed discrepancies and actual similarities. *Journal of Applied Behavioral Science, 29*(4), 416–431. doi:10.1177/0021886393294003

Akgün, A. E., Byrne, J. C., Lynn, G. S., & Keskin, H. (2007). Organizational unlearning as changes in beliefs and routines in organizations. *Journal of Organizational Change Management, 20*(6), 794–812. doi:10.1108/09534810710831028

Albrecht, T. L., & Hall, B. J. (1991). Facilitating talk about new ideas: The role of personal relationships in organizational innovation. *Communication Monographs, 58*(3), 273–288. doi:10.1080/03637759109376230

Anderson, D., & Ackerman Anderson, L. (2001). *Beyond change management: Advanced strategies for today's transformational leaders*. San Francisco, CA: Jossey-Bass/Pfeiffer.

Appelbaum, S. H., & Wohl, L. (2000). Transformation or change: Some prescriptions for health care organizations. *Managing Service Quality, 10*(5), 279–298. doi:10.1108/09604520010345768

Armenakis, A. A., & Harris, S. G. (2009). Reflections: Our journey in organizational change research and practice. *Journal of Change Management, 9*(2), 127–142. doi:10.1080/14697010902879079

Armenakis, A. A., Harris, S. G., & Mossholder, K. W. (1993). Creating readiness for organizational change. *Human Relations, 46*(6), 681–703. doi:10.1177/001872679304600601

Avey, J. B., Wernsing, T. S., & Luthans, F. (2008). Can positive employees help positive organizational change? Impact of psychological capital and emotions on relevant attitudes and behaviors. *Journal of Applied Behavioral Science, 44*(1), 48–70. doi:10.1177/0021886307311470

Ballé, M., & Ballé, F. (2009). *The lean manager: A novel of lean transformation.* Cambridge, MA: Lean Enterprise Institute.

Beer, M., & Nohria, N. (2000). *Breaking the code of change.* Boston, MA: Harvard Business School Press.

Blakley, B. (2012). *Leading lean: Building leadership capacity in the Saskatoon Health Region.* Retrieved from https://student.myrru.royalroads.ca/system/files/groupfiles/bonnie_blakley_olp_edited.pdf

Bridges, W. (1991). *Managing transitions: Making the most of change*. Reading, MA: Addison-Wesley.

Brown, J., & Isaacs, D. (2005). *The world café: Shaping our futures through conversations that matter*. San Francisco, CA: Berrett-Koehler.

Bruckman, J. (2008). Overcoming resistance to change: Causal factors, interventions, and critical values. *The Psychologist – Manager Journal, 11*(2), 211–219. doi:10.1080/10887150802371708

Bunker, B. B., & Alban, B. T. (Eds.). (2006). That was then, but this is now: The past, present, and future of large group methods. In B. B. Bunker & B. T. Albans (Eds.), *The handbook of large group methods: Creating systemic change in organizations and communities*. San Francisco, CA: Jossey-Bass.

Burke, W. W. (2008). *Organization change: Theory and practice* (2nd ed.). Thousand Oaks, CA: Sage.

Burke, W. W., & Litwin, G. H. (2009). A causal model of organizational performance and change. In W. W. Burke, D. G. Lake, & J. W. Paine (Eds.), *Organizational change: A comprehensive reader* (pp. 273–299). San Francisco, CA: Jossey-Bass.

Bushe, G. R. (2012). *Propositions about transforming organizations through dialogic OD.* Retrieved from http://www.gervasebushe.ca/propositions.pdf

Bushe, G. R., & Marshak, R. J. (2009). Revisioning organization development: Diagnostic and dialogic premises and patterns of practice. *Journal of Applied Behavioral Science, 45*, 348–368. doi:10.1177/0021886309335070

Carmeli, A., & Spreitzer, G. (2009). Trust, connectivity, and thriving: Implications for innovative behaviors at work. *Journal of Creative Behavior, 43*(3), 169–191.

Carr, W., & Kemmis, S. (1986). *Becoming critical: Education, knowledge and action research.* London: Falmer Press.

Checkland, P. (1991). From framework through experience to learning: The essential nature of action research. In H. E. Nissen, H. K. Klein, & R. Hirscheim (Eds.), *Information systems research: Contemporary approaches and emergent traditions* (pp. 397–403). Amsterdam: North-Holland/Elsevier Science.

Chin, R., & Benne, K. D. (1961). General strategies for effecting changes in human systems. In W. G. Bennis, K. D. Benne, & R. Chin (Eds.), *The planning of change* (pp. 22–45). Austin, TX: Holt, Rinehart, and Winston.

Coghlan, D., & Brannick, T. (2010). *Doing action research in your own organisation* (3rd ed.). Thousand Oaks, CA: Sage.

Creswell, J. W. (2009). *Research design: Qualitative, quantitative, and mixed methods approaches* (3rd ed.). Thousand Oaks, CA: Sage.

Creswell, J. W., & Plano Clark, V. (2007). *Designing and conducting mixed methods research.* Thousand Oaks, CA: Sage.

Dick, B. (2001). Action research: Action and research. In S. Sankaran, B. Dick, R. Passfield, & P. Swepson (Eds.), *Effective change management using action learning and action research: Concepts, frameworks, processes, applications* (pp. 19–28). Lismore: Southern Cross University Press.

Dickens, L., & Watkins, K. (1999). Action research: Rethinking Lewin. *Management Learning, 30*(2), 127–140. doi:10.1177/1350507699302002

Gardiner, G. G. (2006). Transactional, transformational, and transcendent leadership: Metaphors mapping the evolution of the theory and practice of governance. *Leadership Review*, *6*, 62–76.

Grubbs, B. W. (2001). A community of voices: Using allegory as an interpretive device in action research on organizational change. *Organizational Research Methods, 4*(4), 376–392. doi:10.1177/109442810144004

Gruman, J. A., & Saks, A. M. (2011). Performance management and employee engagement. *Human Resource Management Review, 21*(2), 123–136. doi:10.1016/j.hrmr.2010.09.004

Huy, Q. N., & Mintzberg, H. (2003). The rhythm of change. *MIT Sloan Management Review, 44*(4), 79–84.

Kahn, W. A. (1990). Psychological conditions of personal engagement and disengagement at work. *Academy of Management Journal*, *33*(4), 692–724. doi:10.2307/256287

Kemmis, S., & McTaggart, R. (1995). *The action research planner.* Sydney: Hyperion.

Kenney, C. (2011). *Transforming health care: Virginia Mason Medical Center's pursuit of the perfect patient experience*. New York, NY: Productivity Press.

Kolb, D. (1984). *Experiential learning: Experience as the source of learning and development*. Englewood Cliffs, NJ: Prentice Hall.

Kotter, J. (2007). Leading change, why transformation efforts fail. *Harvard Business Review, 85*(1), 96–103.

Kotter, J. (2012). *Leading change*. Boston, MA: Harvard Business School Press.

Krueger, R., & Casey, M. (2009). *Focus groups: A practical guide for applied research* (4th ed.). Thousand Oaks, CA: Sage.

Lewin, K. (1946). Action research and minority problems. *Journal of Social Issues, 2*(4), 34–46. doi:10.1111/j.1540-4560.1946.tb02295.x

Lewin, K. (Ed.). (1952). *Field theory in social science: Selected theoretical papers*. London: Tavistock.

Lines, R. (2004). Influence of participation in strategic change: Resistance, organizational commitment and change goal achievement. *Journal of Change Management*, *4*(3), 193–215. doi:10.1080/1469701042000221696

London, M., & Sessa, V. I. (2006). Continuous learning in organizations: A living systems analysis of individual, group, and organization learning. In F. J. Yammarino & F. Dansereau (Eds.), *Multi-level issues in social systems*: *Vol 5. Research in multi-level issues* (pp. 123–172). London: Emerald.

Ludema, J. D., Whitney, D., Mohr, B. J., & Griffin, T. J. (2003). *The appreciative inquiry summit: A practitioner's guide for leading large group change*. San Francisco, CA: Berrett-Koehler.

Luthans, F., Avolio, B. J., Avey, J. B., & Norman, S. M. (2007). Positive psychological capital: Measurement and relationship with performance and satisfaction. *Personnel Psychology, 60*, 541–572.

Meaney, M., & Pung, C. (2008, July). McKinsey global survey results: Creating organizational transformations. *The McKinsey Quarterly*, 1–7. Retrieved from http://gsme.sharif.edu/~change/McKinsey Global Survey Results.pdf

National Managers' Community. (2002). *Tools for leadership and learning: Building a learning organization*. Retrieved from http://managers-gestionnaires.gc.ca/documents/toolkit_e.pdf

Owen, H. (1997). *Open space technology: A user's guide* (2nd ed.). San Francisco, CA: Berrett-Koehler.

Piderit, S. K. (2009). Rethinking resistance and recognizing ambivalence: A multidimensional view of the attitudes toward and organizational change. In W. W. Burke, D. G. Lake, & J. W. Paine (Eds.), *Organization change: A comprehensive reader* (pp. 418–439). San Francisco, CA: Jossey-Bass.

Piggot-Irvine, E. (2012). Creating authentic collaboration: A central feature of effectiveness. In O. Zuber-Skerritt (Ed.), *Action research for sustainable development in a turbulent world* (pp. 89–107). Bingley: Emerald.

Piggot-Irvine, E., Connelly, D., Curry, R., Hanna, J., Moodie, M., Palmer, M. . . . Thompson, A. (2011). Building leadership capacity – sustainable leadership. *ALARA Monograph Series*, *2*. Retrieved from http://www.alara.net.au/files/ALARA Monograph No 2 EPiggot-Irvine et al 201109s.pdf

Pochron, S. (2008). Advanced change theory revisited: An article critique. *Integral Review*, *4*(2), 126–132.

Preskill. H., & Torres, R. (1999). *Evaluative inquiry for learning in organizations.* Thousand Oaks, CA: Sage.

Quinn, R. E., Spreitzer, G. M., & Brown, M. V. (2000). Changing others through changing ourselves: The transformation of human systems. *Journal of Management Inquiry*, *9*(2), 147–164. doi:10.1177/105649260092010

Raelin, J. (2012). Dialogue and deliberation as expressions of democratic leadership in participatory organizational change. *Journal of Organizational Change Management,* *25*(1), 7–23. doi:10.1108/09534811211199574

Reason, P., & Bradbury, H. (2001). *Handbook of action research.* Thousand Oaks, CA: Sage.

Robertson, T. (2012). *Fostering employee engagement in the development and engineering services department at the city of [anonymous] to improve customer service*. Unpublished manuscript, School of Leadership Studies, Royal Roads University, Victoria, Canada.

Rowe, W. E., Agger-Gupta, N., Harris, B, & Graf, M. (2011). *Organizational action research (OAR)*. Retrieved from http://student.myrru.royalroads.ca/sites/default/files/oar_diagramv11-2012april19.pdf

Saks, A. M. (2006). Antecedents and consequences of employee engagement. *Journal of Managerial Psychology, 21*(7), 600–619. doi:10.1108/02683940610690169

Sankaran, S., Tay, B. H., & Orr, M. (2009). Managing organizational change by using soft systems thinking in action research projects. *International Journal of Managing Projects in Business, 2*(2), 179–197. doi:10.1108/17538370910949257

Sassenberg, G. (2008). What is lean all about? *CabinetMaker, 22*(1), 36.

Scharmer, C. O. (2009). *Theory U: Learning from the future as it emerges*. San Francisco, CA: Berrett-Koehler.

Schaufeli, W. B., Salanova, M., González-Romá, V., & Bakker, A. B. (2002). The measurement of engagement and burnout: A two sample confirmatory factor analytic approach. *Journal of Happiness Studies, 3*(1), 71–92. doi:10.1023/A:1015630930326

Smith, I. (2006). Continuing professional development and workplace learning – 15: Achieving successful organisational change – do's and don'ts of change management. *Library Management, 27*(4/5), 300–306. doi:10.1108/01435120610668232

Smith, M. L. (2006). Social capital and intentional change: Exploring the role of social networks on individual change efforts. *The Journal of Management Development, 25*(7), 718–731. doi:10.1108/02621710610678517

Stringer, E. T. (2007). *Action research* (3rd ed.). Thousand Oaks, CA: Sage.

Szabla, D. (2007). A multidimensional view of resistance to organizational change: Exploring cognitive, emotional, and intentional responses to planned change across perceived change leadership strategies. *Human Resource Development Quarterly, 18*(4), 525–558. doi:10.1002/hrdq.1218

Torbert, W. (n.d.). *Action inquiry*. Retrieved from http://www.williamrtorbert.com/action-inquiry

Torbert, W. (2004). *Action inquiry: The secret of timely and transforming leadership*. San Francisco, CA: Berrett-Koehler.

Van de Ven, A. H., & Poole, M. S. (2009). Explaining development and change in organizations. In W. W. Burke, D. G. Lake, & J. W. Paine (Eds.), *Organization change: A comprehensive reader* (pp. 859–829). San Francisco, CA: Jossey-Bass.

Wade, S., & Hammick, M. (1999). Action learning circles: Action learning in theory and practice. *Teaching in Higher Education, 4*(2), 163–178. doi:10.1080/1356251990040202

Weisbord, M. R., & Janoff, S. (2000). *Future search: An action guide to finding common group in organizations and communities*. San Francisco, CA: Jossey-Bass/Pleiffer.

Zuber-Skerritt, O. (2002). A model for designing action learning and action research programs. *The Learning Organization, 9*(4), 143–149. doi:10.1108/09696470210428868

Zuber-Skerritt, O. (Ed.). (2012). *Action research for sustainable development in a turbulent world.* Bingley: Emerald.

www.ingramcontent.com/pod-product-compliance
Ingram Content Group UK Ltd.
Pitfield, Milton Keynes, MK11 3LW, UK
UKHW050825070726
13598UKWH00013B/154